Freedom of Spirit
CENTRE OF EXCELLENCE

Published by Freedom of Spirit
14 Park Circus, Glasgow
G3 6AX United Kingdom
Tel 0795 117 2798
Email: freedomofspirit@talktalk.net
www.freedomofspirit.org.uk

A catalogue record for this book is available from the British Library.

Note: The material contained in this book is set out in good faith for general guidance and no liability can be accepted for loss or expense incurred or decisions made as a result of relying in particular circumstances on statements made in the book.

Answers before the questions

by 'Mena'

Spirit speaks again

Introduction

Who is Mena?

Mena is a Spirit Guide who works through medium Tom Anderson. It all started through Tom's trance mediumship when Mena presented himself very clearly. Tom had, for quite some time, been aware of Mena but he had never come forward so verbally before and to such a degree.

Tom had many unusual experiences of Spirit as a child and learned very quickly that it was not always beneficial to mention them, due to people's adverse reaction. He slowly learned to block off these experiences, however, in adulthood they rose again. Tom knew he had work to do for those in Spirit and it was time. Many of his underlying abilities immediately surfaced. The communication lines opened again. He teaches others, along with his wife Linda, how to develop and build that link. Their teachings are of a very high quality and unique.

Mena has a completely different and separate personality from Tom. He has a different way of forming words and presenting himself.

When Tom sits in a relaxed altered state (trance) Mena gives the most wonderful teachings to people, as well as guiding students through deep and powerful meditations. The meditations are literally out of this world. People ask him questions and his answers are not only inspiring, but mind-blowing at times. He is respected and loved by many.

This book began with Tom receiving wonderful quotes which were written down and Tom was asked to compile them in a particular way – a way to benefit everyone.

There are many people who have been invited to hear and benefit from these teachings, which mostly take place in Scotland.

Mena has explained that he used to work through another medium who is now in Spirit. He also stated that "Mena" was not the name he used to identify himself then and does not wish, at this moment in time, to reveal the name he chose to work with in the past. However, some people may connect spirit to spirit when reading this book and recognize Mena's former identity, especially those of a particular spiritual vibration. You will either know or you won't. It is as simple as that. The quotes speak for themselves.

The content and meaning of what is written is what's important and this wonderful book can be read and absorbed again and again. Mena manages to capture the meaning of life in just a few words. He shows the way and draws attention to what is important. He communicates on all levels.

Enjoy this book of quotes as this bright, wise, loving Spirit returns to communicate to the thousands who need his light, his wisdom and his love.

About Tom Anderson

Tom Anderson is certainly the most extraordinary person I have ever known. He is also the most straight talking, honest and spiritual person of this modern day that I will ever meet.

His respect and love of Spirit is commendable and second to none and his ability to change the lives for the better of those around him is remarkable.

Tom goes the extra mile for people and would go from here to eternity for Spirit.

His ability to work with those in Spirit is obvious, but what really shines through is his belief, attitude and his sense of fair play in life. Spirit presents him with amazing teachings and whatever Tom Anderson learns, he teaches others.

He is a pleasure to know, a delight to be around and I can never describe in words how he has changed and touched my life and continues to do so, let alone touch the lives of others. I am not at all surprised that those in Spirit work with him so closely and I am delighted that so do I.

Linda Anderson

The purpose of this book

This book's purpose is to awaken spirituality within you. It is to allow you to think in a way that you may not have been taught.

It gives you the opportunity to create and express your own thoughts, adding them to the book. It enables you to gauge your spiritual development from cover to cover. It's your journey...

People will take from what is written in this book and use it wisely. They will pass the quotes on to others as needed, they may awaken what is lying dormant within them and it is for all these reasons that these words have been written.

This is possibly the most exciting and meaningful book this decade. Is this book perhaps the manuscript of life?

How to use this book

This extraordinary book can be used to stimulate your soul and mind together. It relates to each individual and gives new perspective on emotions, situations and daily life.

You may open this book at a page at random to gain advice or you may ask a question and open a page to discover there you are, presented with your answer. You may read the quote on each page and make your own notes about what the quote means to you. This may allow you to observe your spiritual development, particularly when you look back at what you have written.

These are the jump leads for your spiritual development and as a person emotionally and mentally.

These are the thoughts that send you on your way.

These are the words that make you see the whole of the moon instead of the crescent.

It gives you an answer before you realise that you had a question.

Acknowledgements

I would like to acknowledge Mena my guiding light who is devoted to the spiritual development of the individual. I share his devotion. I would like to thank my wife, Linda Anderson for her support and encouragement throughout.

It's difficult enough to write a book without writing it through mediumship and the views and words of someone else. My wife, as always, was and is beside me in all that I do.

Tom Anderson

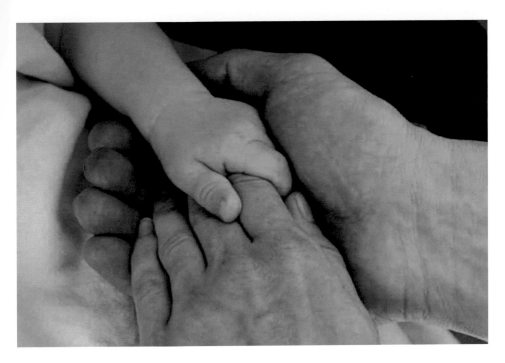

The
power of
love *is* the
power of
spirit.

The power of love

will endeavour to be the life force of which man will ascertain
in his mammoth task of conquering

peace.

If

*in your life time
you walk
five times
round the world,
how far
would you walk*

for Spirit?

If you think the Spirit world is a bridge too far then you will travel many roads to complete your journey.

You
are the lighthouse for the sea of souls.

If you look deep into
your inner self,
you will find
your soul.
Once you
find your soul,
you will
reap the fruits
of the spirit
within.

If we send you the manuscript of life, would you be able to read what is in your *heart?*

When your ship
comes into the harbour,
you
will only be able to disembark if
have evolved.

_____

_____

_____

_____

_____

_____

_____

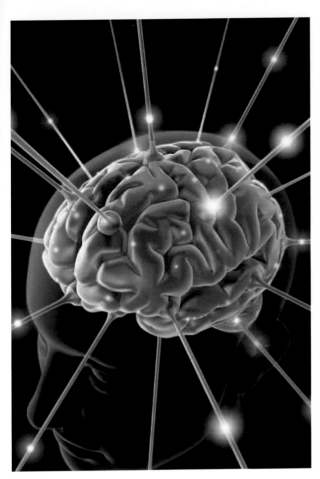

The vast cavern we call **mind** *surpasses all that the* **universe** *has to offer.*

When man begins

his carousel of life
and begins to free
himself from the
deepest dark
within, it is then
that the worker of
light will shine
through.

Yea though you walk through the valley of death, you will fear no evil, for I have never walked through this valley as there is no such place.

The eternal flame
of Spirit will prevail
where the dogmatic life
of man will fail.

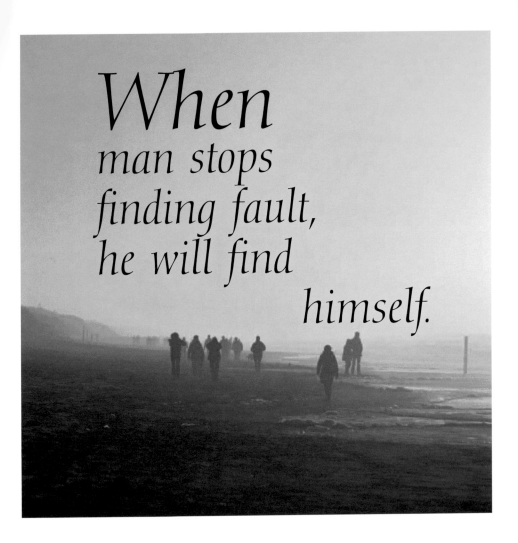

When
man stops
finding fault,
he will find
himself.

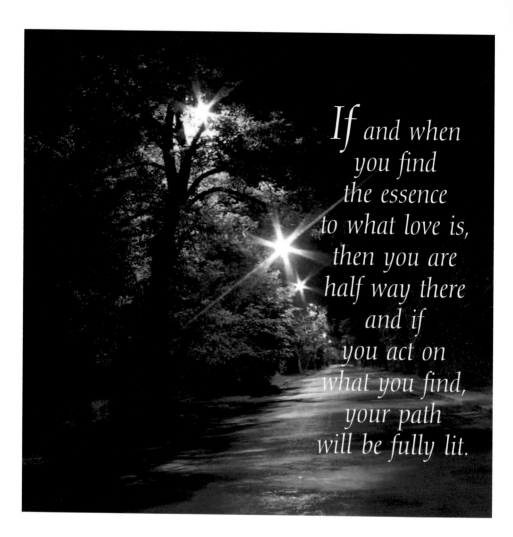

If and when
you find
the essence
to what love is,
then you are
half way there
and if
you act on
what you find,
your path
will be fully lit.

The avalanche of thoughts will only come cascading down on the ever evolving souls whose minds are open to receive.

If a heart
can lead an army
then how can it
be broken with only
one word?

If you think that life is for living, you will. If you think death is for dying, you will. If you think death is for living then you  *know you are on the right path.*

Many have made the transition from death to eternal life but never knew. Many have made the transition of death and knew.
But never have so few made as big an impact on so many.

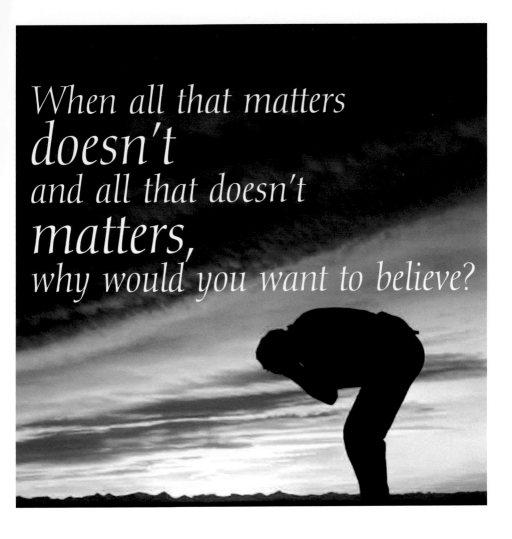

When all that matters
doesn't
and all that doesn't
matters,
why would you want to believe?

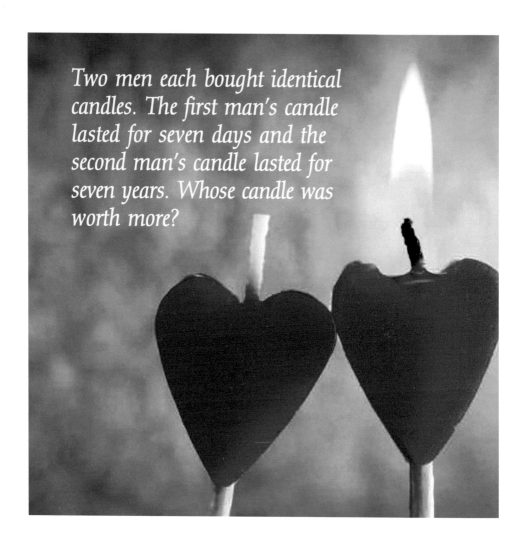

Two men each bought identical candles. The first man's candle lasted for seven days and the second man's candle lasted for seven years. Whose candle was worth more?

If you feel the need to ask if something is true then you have already answered your own question.

*Man
will
eventually*

*invent
himself
out of
work.*

*Many people are looking for answers
to life's problems and looking hard
for solutions, when all they need to do
is look inside themselves.*

When the time comes for you to pass to Spirit, do not think that it is only your wrong doings in the physical sense that matter. Truth is a major ingredient in your manifestation of life, blessed are those who live a life of TRUTH.

Only when man has faced the shame of himself can he go forward in his quest for freedom.

The battleship of
love will one day
muster enough excitement to
conquer the world.

_____

_____

_____

_____

_____

_____

I have never asked and never will ask to be sent back to earth, as it is only when you have felt the sorrow of the passing of a loved one, that you know how much you have travelled on your spiritual journey.

No matter what **harmful** *or nasty acts you muster in your* **material** *life on earth, it is never too late to put that* **feather** *in your cap.*

Mystical, madness, mayhem,

call them what you may, these are only some of the experiences you will endeavour to stumble upon on your journey through the fire coals of life.

Emotions
are only the rollercoaster of life as we know it.

The cheque book of life is where each man has
to pay the price for all of his wrong
doings in his journey through
life and only then will
he be able to
repent.

There is no need for
religion as this is man
made. It is only when
man realises this
 TRUTH that his
life will make
progress in
moving forward.

Success

is not measured by money or status, but by love and truth, thought and action.

Life is not measured by what people say, but how they live and if they were to change the way they live, wouldn't it be a wonderful place?

_____

_____

_____

_____

_____

_____

The guilt
in your
own life
should be
enough.

The merchants of doom will always be the catalyst from which man can never be free of, until he learns that what is in his heart can wage heavily against all that they peddle.

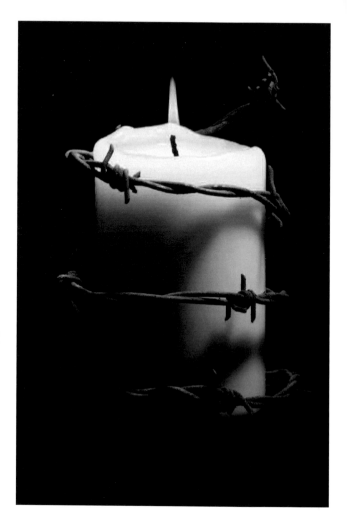

May all you do in life's journey be manipulated with TRUTH. Only then will you make headway in your contemptuous path.

learn from the knowledge within. You are your own master craftsman.

Be your own teacher in life and

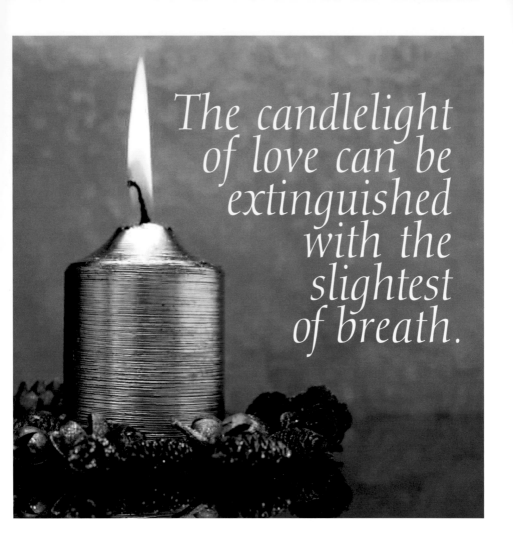

The candlelight
of love can be
extinguished
with the
slightest
of breath.

If helping someone to open a door is a spiritual act, then why does it take man so long to recognise this?

Does man know that when he takes a break from developing on his spiritual journey that it sets him back tenfold and if so, why does he take so many pit stops?

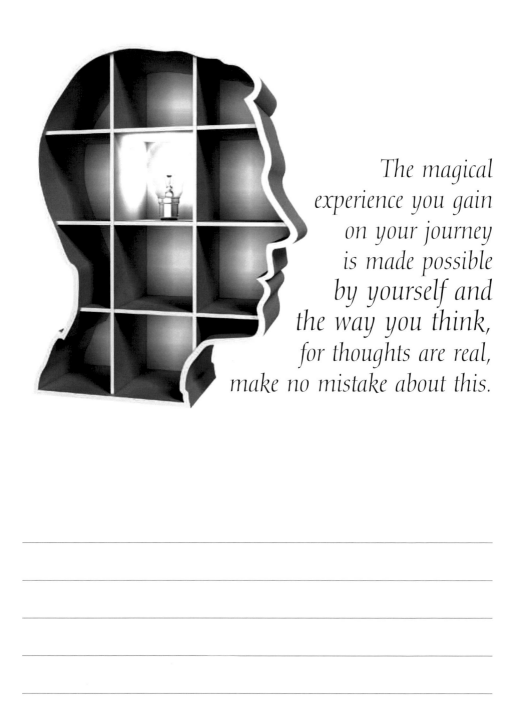

The magical experience you gain on your journey is made possible by yourself and the way you think, for thoughts are real, make no mistake about this.

When you are born unto this earth you are given a mission. Some people learn more quickly than others for everyone receives the same amount of clues all through their life.

If no-one informs you that negativity and guilt will hinder your development, then how would you know differently?

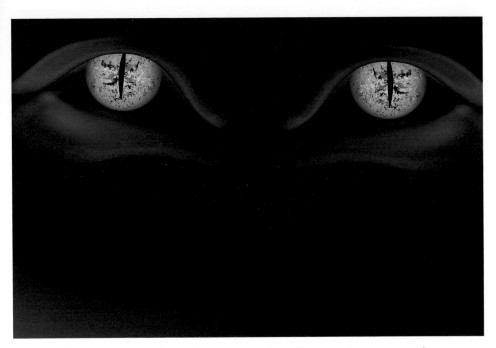

When you look into the burning embers
of a man's eyes you will see his
soul
and once you see his soul you will
know the TRUTH.

No matter what you dream, no matter where you go, it is the actions you take in life that makes your Spirit grow

If your Spirit were to travel from here to the edge of the etheric, would it evolve more than if you were to help someone across a busy road?

If your mind is the
tip of the iceberg,
how much
knowledge do you
think you have?

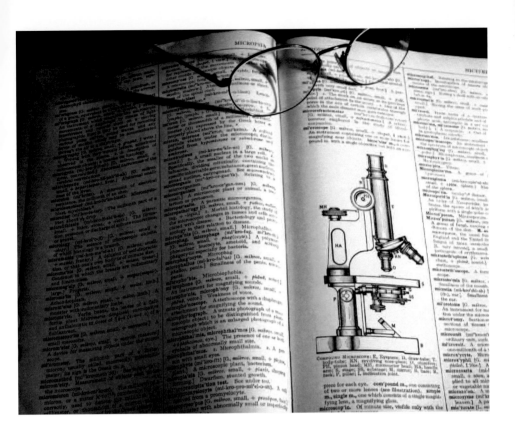

When you look into the dictionary of *life,*
will you be able to decipher what it means?

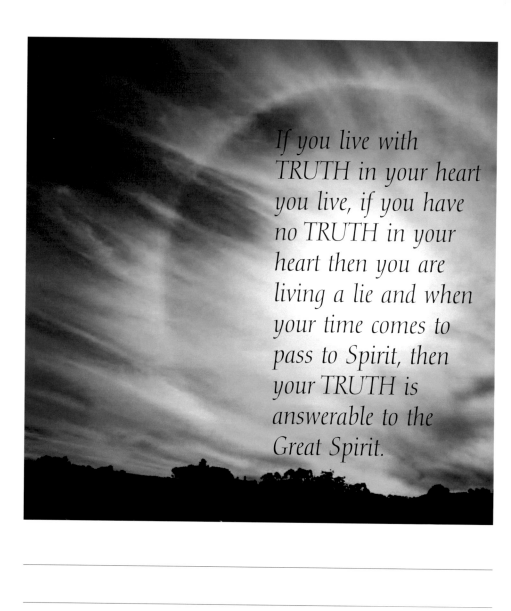

If you live with TRUTH in your heart you live, if you have no TRUTH in your heart then you are living a lie and when your time comes to pass to Spirit, then your TRUTH is answerable to the Great Spirit.

The M.O.T of life-
Measuring
Our
Time.
If you lend your
life to time
then why do you
let yourself go
unchecked?
You would not
let your vehicle go
unchecked after so
much time.

Comparing yourself to your car.

Why would you not drive your car with worn out tyres, yet you
would walk for miles with worn out feet?

Why would you not drive with a damaged chassis, yet you would
bend your damaged back to pick up a weed?

Why would you not drive with your engine sluggish, yet you
would soldier on with a weak heart?

Why would you not drive if your lights were broken, yet you
would not have your eyes checked?

Why would you put more emphasis on your car than on yourself?

When man realises that time has no meaning in the world of Spirit and the importance of how he uses his time in his life, then he will know that this is training for the real thing.

*If thoughts are real
then why is your world
in the* state that it is in?

_____

_____

_____

_____

_____

_____

If TRUTH be the key to all that is good then why is there so much disharmony in man's heart?

The true bond of love surpasses all that is in a man's heart.

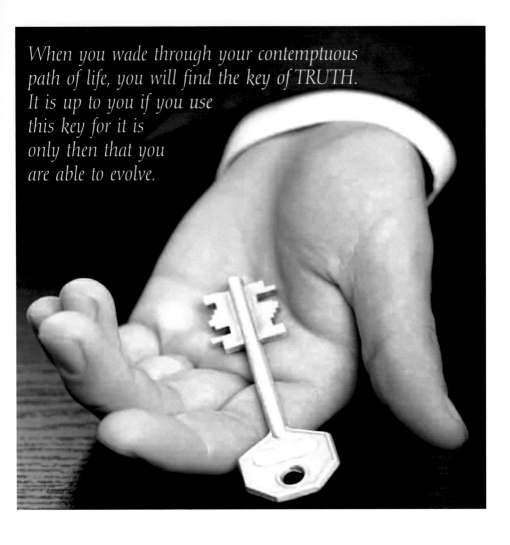

When you wade through your contemptuous path of life, you will find the key of TRUTH. It is up to you if you use this key for it is only then that you are able to evolve.

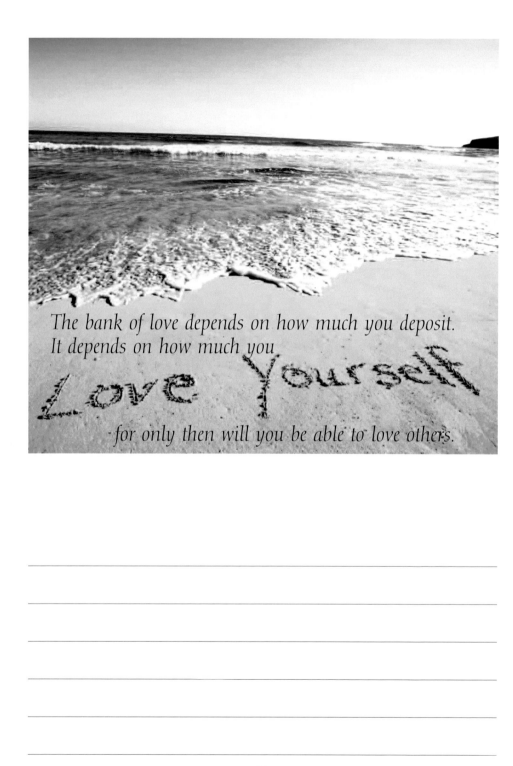

The bank of love depends on how much you deposit.
It depends on how much you *Love Yourself* for only then will you be able to love others.

_____

_____

_____

_____

_____

*Self
indulgence
is a
very rare
commodity.*

Why does man expect to have an easy path through his life when he has already laid the hidden mines?

If you could paint a picture of your life,
how would your picture look and do you believe you are
the star
in your own life?

_____

_____

_____

_____

_____

_____

Your pathway through life can be as wide and as narrow as you wish it to be.

_____

_____

_____

_____

_____

If you had the choice to be someone else, would you and would your reasons be correct?

The level of TRUTH in a man's life is very important for it is in this TRUTH that you will be judged and therefore will decipher which level you attain to when you pass to the Spirit world.

In your quest for riches, glory, power and possessions in your life, do you ever stop and ask yourself why?

Always be the
king or
queen in your own life,
never the
pawn.

*Considering
the fact that quantum
does exist, isn't it a pity that
more people do not believe
in the other worlds?*

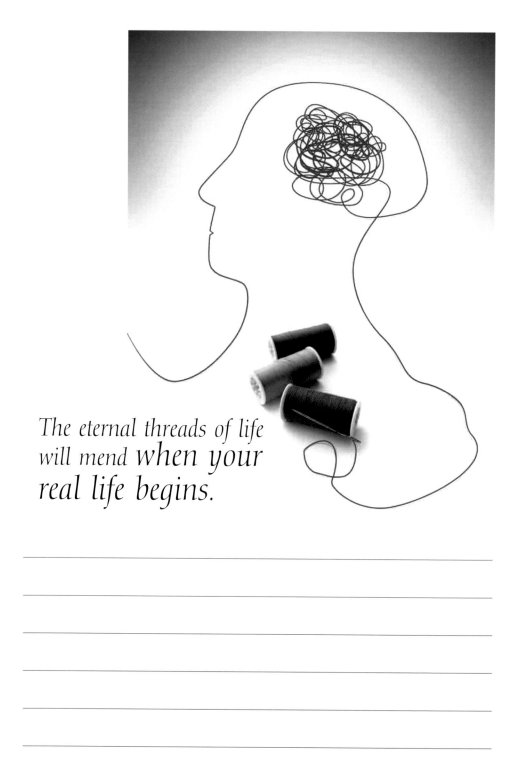

The eternal threads of life
will mend *when your*
real life begins.

The seasons of life are the same to all men
and when winter ends, spring begins.

When you live your life like roulette, then why does it surprise you when things don't go to plan?

The fountain of love will anodise deep within your heart when you are ready to receive it. It is then you will know what tunnel your journey will take, for not everyone goes through the same tunnel.

The seasons of our lives

Our lives begin when we are born (Spring) from puberty to adulthood (Summer), from young adulthood to mid adulthood (Autumn) until you reach your Winter, which is different for each of us.

It is then you return to spring.

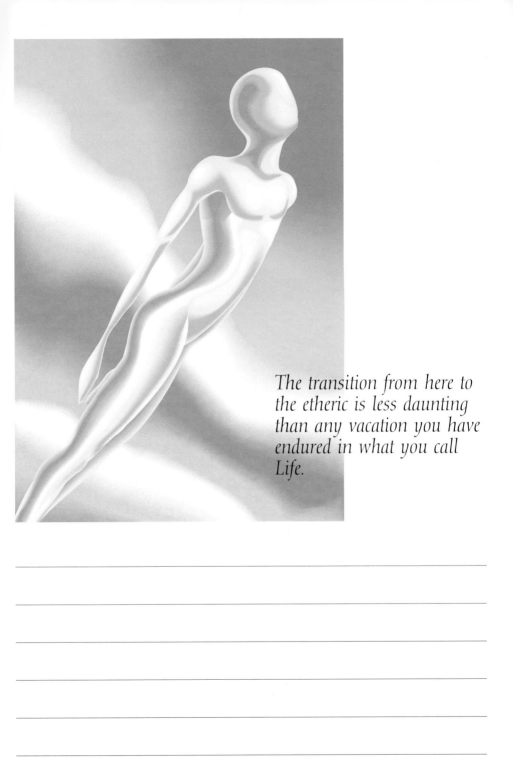

The transition from here to the etheric is less daunting than any vacation you have endured in what you call Life.

*If TRUTH
was money
and riches,
how rich
would
your life be?*

The helium of guilt will
always weigh heavily in
man's heart, for it is only
when his TRUTHS are told
will the guilt lighten and
float away.

When your boat of life trawls it's
way through the dogmatic waves,
it will be then that you will
understand just how your
development can and
will be made
clearer.

In that jungle you call Life, if you live the life of the lion you will receive all you need and if you live the life of a loner you will achieve nothing.

When your time comes to pass
through the etheric
into the angelic
realms of the Spirit
world, it is then
that the Life you
have lived will
be rewound and
played back for
you to judge, as you
are your own judge and jury.

If you live your life like the eagle

then you will gain the wisdom which will guide
you through the flight of your journey, the
TRUTH within and the knowledge to survive.

_____

_____

_____

_____

_____

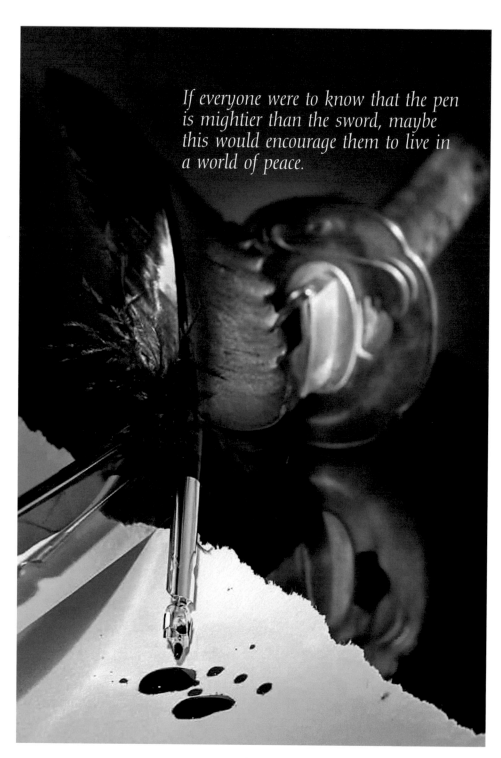

If everyone were to know that the pen is mightier than the sword, maybe this would encourage them to live in a world of peace.

If you look for the negative in people you will find it. If you look for good you may find it. If you look for the TRUTH in people you will need to look very hard.

When man judges his neighbour he judges himself, for only when he can judge himself will he see the TRUTH.

If you have lived your life by the orthodox religions bestowed upon you, why does it surprise you when you pass to Spirit that you have not evolved, unless of course you lived it with LOVE and TRUTH.

With the onslaught of success man faces a tribunal of hate and venom from mankind. It is only when he realises this misadventure that the Great Spirit can penetrate the mind and install the TRUTH of life and evolution.

*When
the crusade
of life
marches
forward
and enters
your
path,*

*it is
then
that
you will
know
what
your life
journey's
path is.*

If when you are born is the
beginning of your journey home,
wouldn't it be a long journey without the
knowledge of progression and an understanding of

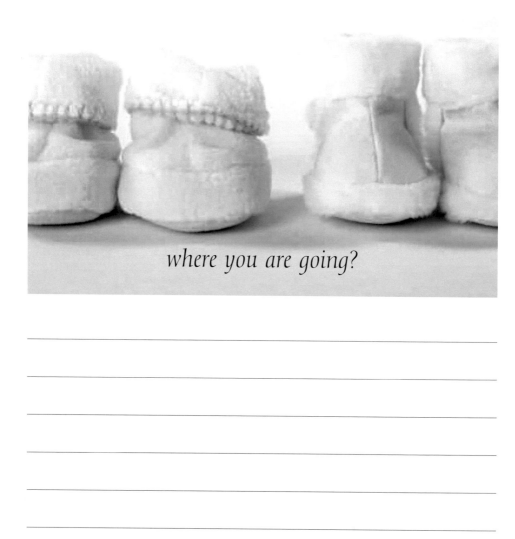

where you are going?

*Your inner light
will only ignite when
you are ready to begin
your quest for knowledge
and it is only then you
will advance in your
spiritual path of
enlightenment.*

Many have started their path of TRUTH but faltered badly when the ego pushed into that path. It does not matter how many times you start your path of TRUTH as long as you learn along the way.

When you kick start someone else's journey for them it catapults you forward in your own path of enlightenment more that you will ever know.

If TRUTH is stronger than religion, then why does it take so long for man to realise that he is on the wrong path or does he think it is only his religion that will lead him to the Great Spirit?

*When all you need
to develop is in front
of you, why do you
waste time looking
for something you
already have and
when you find what
you are looking for,
why do you fall at
the first hurdle?*

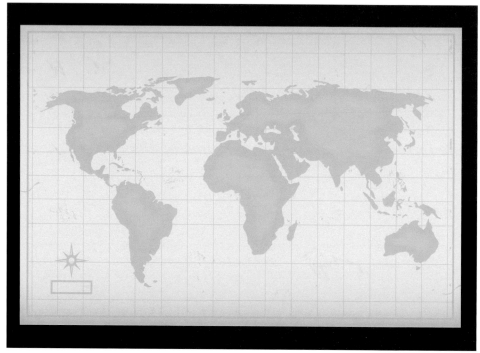

When the map of TRUTH is set out in front of you why is it so hard to read, or is it simply that you are still finding your way?

The eternal light of Life will always be lit within. It can be as bright or as dim as you make it, for it is the belief and TRUTH that you have in your heart that powers this light.

Why, when you can manifest your own destiny, does man always rely on what others say, even when the thoughts that he has in his own mind can change the world?

_____

_____

_____

_____

_____

You will know that you believe in the Great Spirit when, in your time of need,

you ask for help and you receive it.

Why does man believe so much in what he reads when all he has done is believe in another man's *opinion?*

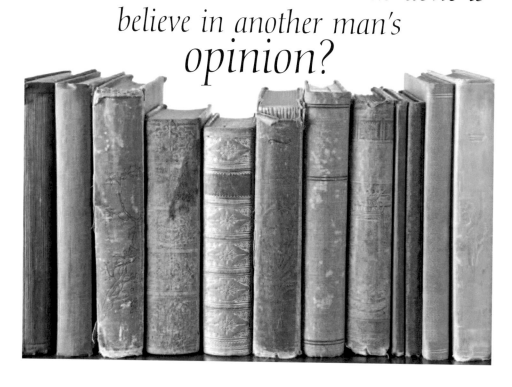

When you love from the heart you can achieve all that you
need in life.

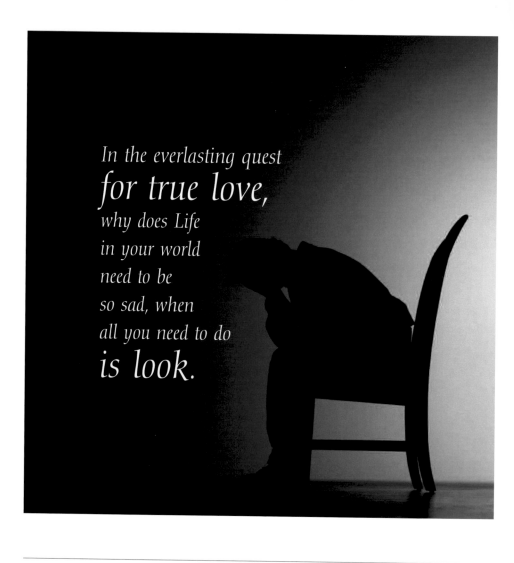

In the everlasting quest
for true love,
why does Life
in your world
need to be
so sad, when
all you need to do
is look.

May all you do in your life be done in love, for love will light your path to the fullest. Your love will help heal the world and lift many who have fallen on their path, as love is the law of the Universe.

When you awaken from within
and realise the reason for Life, you will
find what awaits you as you are ready
to receive it, the abundance of Spirit
that is perfect. The fact is that once you
receive this, it cannot be lost. The rewards
for your work, the enlightenment of
your soul within, it will be then that you see

the real light that lights your path in Life.

Conclusion

*The most important words to remember
while working with Spirit are;
LOVE, HONESTY, SINCERITY and TRUTH.*

LOVE is a word that is used by many very loosely. They will say the word, but do not know it's meaning. It is important to find love in your heart for without love you will never evolve. It can be love of a partner and returned to you (maximum strength), it can be the love for an animal as they offer unconditional love (very strong). However, the most important love of all is the love for oneself, for without this you cannot love anything.

HONESTY is a word that is used to get the attention of others and to get them out of trouble, but honesty should be used without force.

SINCERITY is a very important word as the sincerity you have makes a difference in whether you live your life to the full.

TRUTH I have saved this word for last, as it is at the end of one's life that is affected. If you have not lived a life of TRUTH you will not evolve, therefore you will be on a lower level, for TRUTH will determine which level you achieve. Be aware of TRUTH.